Beautiful Mistakes

by rj avenira

rj avenira

rj avenira

rj avenira

rj avenira

dedicated to the true
souls
who reach to the stars
and know their worth

rj avenira

rj avenira

CHAPTERS

1.   open wounds
2.   broken souls
3.   cloudy days
4. beautiful mistakes

chapter one

rj avenira

open wounds

broken promises
leave scarred soil
across the fields
of your heart

but one day
you will heal
and plant anew

with or without
their reassurance
you remain
valuable beyond words

those who tell you
'i love you'
will be the ones
to hurt you
the most

it is not easy
to forget
the wounds
that still ache
within you

but fear not
one day
you will find
your healing

we lit up that
cigarette
and looked out the
window
into the starry
night's sky

love found us aching
hoping for something
more

love found us
in the middle of the
night

pain is the thing that
teaches you
the places
you need to be held
tenderly
by someone
who truly loves you

there have been men
who have wanted you
and sworn
they were ready
to play with fire

but they
were too weak
to handle
your flame

do not be
so hard
on yourself

life is rife with
struggle
you cannot blame
yourself
for needing rest

all those who hurt you
will be the first
to crawl back
to you

once you have found
your healing

your heart
remembers the days
of light and love
with fond nostalgia

but put yourself at
ease

you have
still better days
waiting for you

what really matters
is that you never
believe
that you deserve
to be treated
the way they treat you

do not hesitate
to say no
to the things
and people
in your life
that infringe
on your peace

we were too young and
lost to understand the
love that ignited such
a fire in our souls

perhaps one day our
paths will cross again

and everything will
fit together in such
beautiful ways as we
cannot even imagine

you are plagued
with those
in your life
who do nothing
but take your love
and give nothing back

you deserve
to be surrounded
with people
who reflect your light
instead of taking it
all
for themselves

i was never
your first priority

you saw me as an
option
and i saw you
as my only

and that is why
we caused each other
nothing but pain

love
is a beautiful thing

but even love
can cause us pain

as we are forever lost
in pursuit
of something
that feels real

you are laying your
heart
at the feet of men
who are willing
to trod over it
carelessly
just to get
to another woman

do not give your time
to people
who believe
that you owe them
anything

do not ignore
the ache in your heart
that demands
to be heard

all of these
broken things
will one day
add up
to a wholeness
you cannot
even imagine

everything
you need
is already
inside
yourself

there is no better
feeling
than to have
your heart
in harmony
with your spirit

but all too often
in life
that is a feeling
we seldom feel

do not compare
yourself
to the fake perfection
that others present

give your sadness
the attention
it deserves

do not run away
from confronting
your feelings

do not fear chaos
become the storm
and there
you will find
your power

there is a difference
between forgiving
people
and giving them
another chance
to make the same
mistakes
they made before

the day will come
where all of the
concerns which plague
your heart at this
moment will be as
forgotten as the
weather a decade ago
on this day.

take heart in this:
things will change
and your heart will
heal
one day at a time

i have come a long way
from the poverty
of unpaid
electricity bills
and sitting
in the darkness

ironically
it was
talking about my pain
after so much time
of holding it in
that brought me out
of the darkness

-blood on my
typewriter

beautiful is the rose
that stands strong
despite
the strongest winds

do not let the world
make you
stop caring

if you fed a flower
nothing but
alcohol
and cigarettes
how could it still
bloom?

and yet
here i am
on my journey
forward

rj avenira

rj avenira

33

chapter two

rj avenira

broken souls

broken souls
always
find each other
in the darkness

you can't blame
yourself
for losing
who you are
while you
were so focused
on trying
to help him

it's not your job
to fix a man
who was not
raised well

be careful
who you speak to
when they
are careless
with the secrets
of others

i have slowly
become okay
with the fact
that you
will never explain
what happened
between us

do not be
with someone
who will not accept
any blame
for what they do
or say

i needed you
more
than you
ever
needed me

imbalance
is the root
of heartbreak

you don't need
a man
to validate
who you are

draw your strength
from deep within

do not let the world
make you feel
weak

i know that you
have been forced
to raise yourself
because you
never had
any good examples
to draw from

you should be proud
of every inch
you have gained
in ground
from where
you began

if you've never
thought
about killing someone
you don't really
love them

trust is a loaded gun
that you put
into the hands
of someone else

you deserve someone
who stays

sometimes
you just have to cry
until you
are so exhausted
that you
can begin
to move on

the moment
we begin
to become jealous
is the moment
we give
all our power
to the worst parts
of the other person

if you are happier
without you

then i
want you
to leave me

whiskey
is no cure
for the pain

but it can dull it
for the night

someone
who does not show you
that they care

doesn't

whisper things to me
deep in the night
comfort
my weary soul
promise me
things
we could never keep

lust
when it goes
both ways

can feel
close to love

rj avenira

i envy
the rain
as it falls
and touches
your body

sex
is not a dirty word

we cannot rush things
and make them happen
before
they are meant to

that
is as unfulfilling
as harvesting
the fruit
before it is ripe

in the end
you cannot afford
to let someone else
be your peace

if you rely
on someone else
to comfort your heart
it will only hurt
all the more
when they
recoil away
when things get tough

you see my past
and see
something
to be afraid of

the right person
will not
recoil
from your flaws

find someone
who knows
that no one else
can replace
the beauty
of your soul

do not come to me
asking for forgiveness
when i have not
even had time
to forgive myself
for giving you
a chance

rj avenira

chapter three

rj avenira

cloudy days

the clouds
cover the sun
but they
are not
immortal

they will fade away
one day
just as your struggle
will one day
just be
another chapter
in the story
of your past

do not think
that just because
he called you
special
that means
he believes it

find someone
whose kindness
of heart
matches the kindness
of their words

come with me

let's set fire
to the last
of everything
we still
hold on to

let's start fresh
without scars
without expectations
let's leave everything
behind

he will regret
losing you

but do not
fall back
into his arms

let his mistake
of losing a diamond
be your chance
to realize
that you
deserve
so much more
than him

i was sipping wine
sitting on the porch
deep into the night
a notebook in hand
trying to write

but all
i could think about
was you

you will be the one
he regrets losing
more than any
of the others

do not let anyone
come and go
into your life
as they please

you are more
than an option

be careful
where you plant
yourself

even the seeds
of a beautiful rose
when planted
on the rocks
will produce nothing
but pain

do not spend your
nights
wasting time
thinking
about where he is
and who
he is with

you cannot
start a new chapter
in your life
while you
are still holding on
to someone
who moved on
from you
a long time ago

in a world
where mirages of
beauty
pass for the real
thing
you are one of the few
who are real
and true

do not allow
his cold heart
to take your warmth
and make you
like him

he does not deserve
the energy
you give him

you are far too
powerful

too full
of lightning
sprung from the hands
of goddesses

to think
that some lowly man
is worthy
of the grieving
of your heart

one day
you will realize
that all of your
waiting
and mistakes
were leading
to a future
of abundant happiness

the clouds
obscure the sun
but she
is planning
her revenge
and will dissipate
them all
in the morning
with her first touch

it is okay
to outgrow people

we made a language
all our own
out of the slang
and ways of speaking
that we formed
together

the sun knows
that the whims
of the clouds
on earth

truly mean nothing
in the larger scheme
of things

she will win
in the end

everyone deserves
to exist
exactly as they are

nice guys
who are just
using being 'nice'
as a way
to try to get sex
are the worst
type of men

we are all
just trying to find
our place
in this world

life
is far too short
not to take
everything
it has to offer

do not listen
to those
who tell you
that you
must change
who you are

rj avenira

love
always wins

you showed me
the type of love
that my analytical
mind
could only
begin to appreciate

rj avenira

&

chapter four

rj avenira

beautiful mistakes

the greatest secret
of life
is that we
are the product
of the mistakes
we make

mistakes shape us
into the person
we will ultimately
become

rj avenira

love
will put you
back together

stop losing sleep
over those
who don't even
bat an eye
at the idea
that they
have hurt you

your inner fire
is enough
to devour the world

do not
treat it lightly

to be broken
is not the same
as giving up

you do not need
to give up

on the contrary

see this as an
opportunity
to put yourself
back together again
into something
new

you do not know
the extent
of your true strength
until
you keep fighting
even though
you're tired

keep going
even when
it seems
like the most
impossible thing
in the entire world

the best part
about healing
is that your scars
make you stronger
than you've ever been
before

you will know
that your strength
has eclipsed
your pain
when you find yourself
capable
of moving on

rj avenira

every beautiful thing
comes from pain

a dove
cannot take to the
skies
without going
through the struggle
of breaking through
its shell

once
you have begun
to heal yourself

your inner light
will spread
to those around you

it is time
to tell your heart
to move on

find someone
who doesn't cringe
when you express
your individuality
and quirks

find someone
who sees who you are
and loves you deeply

be ruthless
with cutting out
the things
and people
in your life
that don't make you

happy

do not feel guilty
for cutting out
the people
who add stress
and negative energy
into your life

let the toxic people
go

i swear
the power of your soul
is infinite

do not think twice
about leaving
situations
that make you
feel
badly
about yourself

some people just want
to hurt you to make
themselves feel a
sense of power that
they do not deserve

do not take it
personally
but also
do not
give them a pass
for the way they act

ultimately
the person
you need most
in the world
is yourself

rj avenira

focus on yourself
first and foremost

no matter
the length
of your journey
do not forget
to keep
looking up

the cosmos
move
in their beautiful
patterns
within the confines
of your soul

you do not need
to hold yourself
to the standard
of perfection

it is enough
to push further
than you were
yesterday

do not allow others
to take
your inner light
from you

joy
is a beautiful thing
on the face
of a woman
who has gotten over
a man
who does not
deserve her

rj avenira

your problems
are not permanent

you will look back
on them one day

feeling free
as a bird
having conquered
all

you
were my
most beautiful
mistake

rj avenira

rj avenira

<u>also by rj avenira</u>

blood on my typewriter

rj avenira

Beautiful Mistakes

Beautiful Mistakes is
a book of poetry by
bestselling author rj
avenira. it expands
from the brutal
honesty of his last
book to look the
darkness of life &
heartbreak in the eyes
and swear to move on.

this is a journey of
love, heartbreak,
hope, and healing.

Made in the USA
Monee, IL
09 May 2020